If Lost, Please Return This Brew Logbook To:

_____

Index Of Recipes

	Brew Name	Page

Index Of Recipes

	Brew Name	Page

RECIPE NAME

BREW DATE	BOTTLING/KEG DATE
STYLE	RECIPE SIZE
ORIGINAL GRAVITY	BITTERNESS (IBUs)
FINAL GRAVITY	COLOR (SRM)
BATCH SIZE	BATCH TYPE
ALCOHOL (ABV)	EFFICIENCY

INGREDIENTS

AMT	GRAIN/EXTRACT	ANT (Oz/g)	HOPS	TIME	% AA	IBU

Yeast Strain_____# of Packets_____

BOIL

WEIGHT	HOPS/BOIL INGREDIENTS	AAUs	IBUs	TIME

FERMENTATION

DATE	STEP (Primary, Secondary)	START TEMP	END TEMP	# OF DAYS

DATE	FERMENTATION ADDITION (Dry Hop/Fruit/Etc.)	AMOUNT	# OF DAYS

BREWING NOTES

RECIPE NAME

BREW DATE	BOTTLING/KEG DATE
STYLE	RECIPE SIZE
ORIGINAL GRAVITY	BITTERNESS (IBUs)
FINAL GRAVITY	COLOR (SRM)
BATCH SIZE	BATCH TYPE
ALCOHOL (ABV)	EFFICIENCY

INGREDIENTS

AMT	GRAIN/EXTRACT	ANT (Oz/g)	HOPS	TIME	% AA	IBU

Yeast Strain_____# of Packets_____

BOIL

WEIGHT	HOPS/BOIL INGREDIENTS	AAUs	IBUs	TIME

FERMENTATION

DATE	STEP (Primary, Secondary)	START TEMP	END TEMP	# OF DAYS

DATE	FERMENTATION ADDITION (Dry Hop/Fruit/Etc.)	AMOUNT	# OF DAYS

BREWING NOTES

RECIPE NAME

BREW DATE	BOTTLING/KEG DATE
STYLE	RECIPE SIZE
ORIGINAL GRAVITY	BITTERNESS (IBUs)
FINAL GRAVITY	COLOR (SRM)
BATCH SIZE	BATCH TYPE
ALCOHOL (ABV)	EFFICIENCY

INGREDIENTS

AMT	GRAIN/EXTRACT	ANT (Oz/g)	HOPS	TIME	% AA	IBU

Yeast Strain_____# of Packets_____

BOIL

WEIGHT	HOPS/BOIL INGREDIENTS	AAUs	IBUs	TIME

FERMENTATION

DATE	STEP (Primary, Secondary)	START TEMP	END TEMP	# OF DAYS

DATE	FERMENTATION ADDITION (Dry Hop/Fruit/Etc.)	AMOUNT	# OF DAYS

BREWING NOTES

RECIPE NAME

BREW DATE	BOTTLING/KEG DATE
STYLE	RECIPE SIZE
ORIGINAL GRAVITY	BITTERNESS (IBUs)
FINAL GRAVITY	COLOR (SRM)
BATCH SIZE	BATCH TYPE
ALCOHOL (ABV)	EFFICIENCY

INGREDIENTS

AMT	GRAIN/EXTRACT	ANT (Oz/g)	HOPS	TIME	% AA	IBU

Yeast Strain_____# of Packets_____

BOIL

WEIGHT	HOPS/BOIL INGREDIENTS	AAUs	IBUs	TIME

FERMENTATION

DATE	STEP (Primary, Secondary)	START TEMP	END TEMP	# OF DAYS

DATE	FERMENTATION ADDITION (Dry Hop/Fruit/Etc.)	AMOUNT	# OF DAYS

BREWING NOTES

RECIPE NAME

BREW DATE	BOTTLING/KEG DATE
STYLE	RECIPE SIZE
ORIGINAL GRAVITY	BITTERNESS (IBUs)
FINAL GRAVITY	COLOR (SRM)
BATCH SIZE	BATCH TYPE
ALCOHOL (ABV)	EFFICIENCY

INGREDIENTS

AMT	GRAIN/EXTRACT	ANT (Oz/g)	HOPS	TIME	% AA	IBU

Yeast Strain_____# of Packets_____

BOIL

WEIGHT	HOPS/BOIL INGREDIENTS	AAUs	IBUs	TIME

FERMENTATION

DATE	STEP (Primary, Secondary)	START TEMP	END TEMP	# OF DAYS

DATE	FERMENTATION ADDITION (Dry Hop/Fruit/Etc.)	AMOUNT	# OF DAYS

BREWING NOTES

RECIPE NAME

BREW DATE	BOTTLING/KEG DATE
STYLE	RECIPE SIZE
ORIGINAL GRAVITY	BITTERNESS (IBUs)
FINAL GRAVITY	COLOR (SRM)
BATCH SIZE	BATCH TYPE
ALCOHOL (ABV)	EFFICIENCY

INGREDIENTS

AMT	GRAIN/EXTRACT	AMT (Oz/g)	HOPS	TIME	% AA	IBU

Yeast Strain_____# of Packets_____

BOIL

WEIGHT	HOPS/BOIL INGREDIENTS	AAUs	IBUs	TIME

FERMENTATION

DATE	STEP (Primary, Secondary)	START TEMP	END TEMP	# OF DAYS

DATE	FERMENTATION ADDITION (Dry Hop/Fruit/Etc.)	AMOUNT	# OF DAYS

BREWING NOTES

RECIPE NAME

BREW DATE	BOTTLING/KEG DATE
STYLE	RECIPE SIZE
ORIGINAL GRAVITY	BITTERNESS (IBUs)
FINAL GRAVITY	COLOR (SRM)
BATCH SIZE	BATCH TYPE
ALCOHOL (ABV)	EFFICIENCY

INGREDIENTS

AMT	GRAIN/EXTRACT	ANT (Oz/g)	HOPS	TIME	% AA	IBU

Yeast Strain_____# of Packets_____

BOIL

WEIGHT	HOPS/BOIL INGREDIENTS	AAUs	IBUs	TIME

FERMENTATION

DATE	STEP (Primary, Secondary)	START TEMP	END TEMP	# OF DAYS

DATE	FERMENTATION ADDITION (Dry Hop/Fruit/Etc.)	AMOUNT	# OF DAYS

BREWING NOTES

RECIPE NAME

BREW DATE	BOTTLING/KEG DATE
STYLE	RECIPE SIZE
ORIGINAL GRAVITY	BITTERNESS (IBUs)
FINAL GRAVITY	COLOR (SRM)
BATCH SIZE	BATCH TYPE
ALCOHOL (ABV)	EFFICIENCY

INGREDIENTS

AMT	GRAIN/EXTRACT	ANT (Oz/g)	HOPS	TIME	% AA	IBU

Yeast Strain_____# of Packets_____

BOIL

WEIGHT	HOPS/BOIL INGREDIENTS	AAUs	IBUs	TIME

FERMENTATION

DATE	STEP (Primary, Secondary)	START TEMP	END TEMP	# OF DAYS

DATE	FERMENTATION ADDITION (Dry Hop/Fruit/Etc.)	AMOUNT	# OF DAYS

BREWING NOTES

RECIPE NAME

BREW DATE	BOTTLING/KEG DATE
STYLE	RECIPE SIZE
ORIGINAL GRAVITY	BITTERNESS (IBUs)
FINAL GRAVITY	COLOR (SRM)
BATCH SIZE	BATCH TYPE
ALCOHOL (ABV)	EFFICIENCY

INGREDIENTS

AMT	GRAIN/EXTRACT	ANT (Oz/g)	HOPS	TIME	% AA	IBU

Yeast Strain_____# of Packets_____

BOIL

WEIGHT	HOPS/BOIL INGREDIENTS	AAUs	IBUs	TIME

FERMENTATION

DATE	STEP (Primary, Secondary)	START TEMP	END TEMP	# OF DAYS

DATE	FERMENTATION ADDITION (Dry Hop/Fruit/Etc.)	AMOUNT	# OF DAYS

BREWING NOTES

RECIPE NAME

BREW DATE	BOTTLING/KEG DATE
STYLE	RECIPE SIZE
ORIGINAL GRAVITY	BITTERNESS (IBUs)
FINAL GRAVITY	COLOR (SRM)
BATCH SIZE	BATCH TYPE
ALCOHOL (ABV)	EFFICIENCY

INGREDIENTS

AMT	GRAIN/EXTRACT	AMT (Oz/g)	HOPS	TIME	% AA	IBU

Yeast Strain_____# of Packets_____

BOIL

WEIGHT	HOPS/BOIL INGREDIENTS	AAUs	IBUs	TIME

FERMENTATION

DATE	STEP (Primary, Secondary)	START TEMP	END TEMP	# OF DAYS

DATE	FERMENTATION ADDITION (Dry Hop/Fruit/Etc.)	AMOUNT	# OF DAYS

BREWING NOTES

RECIPE NAME

BREW DATE	BOTTLING/KEG DATE
STYLE	RECIPE SIZE
ORIGINAL GRAVITY	BITTERNESS (IBUs)
FINAL GRAVITY	COLOR (SRM)
BATCH SIZE	BATCH TYPE
ALCOHOL (ABV)	EFFICIENCY

INGREDIENTS

AMT	GRAIN/EXTRACT	ANT (Oz/g)	HOPS	TIME	% AA	IBU

Yeast Strain_____# of Packets_____

BOIL

WEIGHT	HOPS/BOIL INGREDIENTS	AAUs	IBUs	TIME

FERMENTATION

DATE	STEP (Primary, Secondary)	START TEMP	END TEMP	# OF DAYS

DATE	FERMENTATION ADDITION (Dry Hop/Fruit/Etc.)	AMOUNT	# OF DAYS

BREWING NOTES

RECIPE NAME

BREW DATE		BOTTLING/KEG DATE	
STYLE		RECIPE SIZE	
ORIGINAL GRAVITY		BITTERNESS (IBUs)	
FINAL GRAVITY		COLOR (SRM)	
BATCH SIZE		BATCH TYPE	
ALCOHOL (ABV)		EFFICIENCY	

INGREDIENTS

AMT	GRAIN/EXTRACT	ANT (Oz/g)	HOPS	TIME	% AA	IBU

Yeast Strain_____# of Packets_____

BOIL

WEIGHT	HOPS/BOIL INGREDIENTS	AAUs	IBUs	TIME

FERMENTATION

DATE	STEP (Primary, Secondary)	START TEMP	END TEMP	# OF DAYS

DATE	FERMENTATION ADDITION (Dry Hop/Fruit/Etc.)	AMOUNT	# OF DAYS

BREWING NOTES

RECIPE NAME

BREW DATE	BOTTLING/KEG DATE
STYLE	RECIPE SIZE
ORIGINAL GRAVITY	BITTERNESS (IBUs)
FINAL GRAVITY	COLOR (SRM)
BATCH SIZE	BATCH TYPE
ALCOHOL (ABV)	EFFICIENCY

INGREDIENTS

AMT	GRAIN/EXTRACT	ANT (Oz/g)	HOPS	TIME	% AA	IBU

Yeast Strain_____# of Packets_____

BOIL

WEIGHT	HOPS/BOIL INGREDIENTS	AAUs	IBUs	TIME

FERMENTATION

DATE	STEP (Primary, Secondary)	START TEMP	END TEMP	# OF DAYS

DATE	FERMENTATION ADDITION (Dry Hop/Fruit/Etc.)	AMOUNT	# OF DAYS

BREWING NOTES

RECIPE NAME

BREW DATE	BOTTLING/KEG DATE
STYLE	RECIPE SIZE
ORIGINAL GRAVITY	BITTERNESS (IBUs)
FINAL GRAVITY	COLOR (SRM)
BATCH SIZE	BATCH TYPE
ALCOHOL (ABV)	EFFICIENCY

INGREDIENTS

AMT	GRAIN/EXTRACT	ANT (Oz/g)	HOPS	TIME	% AA	IBU

Yeast Strain_____# of Packets_____

BOIL

WEIGHT	HOPS/BOIL INGREDIENTS	AAUs	IBUs	TIME

FERMENTATION

DATE	STEP (Primary, Secondary)	START TEMP	END TEMP	# OF DAYS

DATE	FERMENTATION ADDITION (Dry Hop/Fruit/Etc.)	AMOUNT	# OF DAYS

BREWING NOTES

RECIPE NAME

BREW DATE	BOTTLING/KEG DATE
STYLE	RECIPE SIZE
ORIGINAL GRAVITY	BITTERNESS (IBUs)
FINAL GRAVITY	COLOR (SRM)
BATCH SIZE	BATCH TYPE
ALCOHOL (ABV)	EFFICIENCY

INGREDIENTS

AMT	GRAIN/EXTRACT	ANT (Oz/g)	HOPS	TIME	% AA	IBU

Yeast Strain_____# of Packets_____

BOIL

WEIGHT	HOPS/BOIL INGREDIENTS	AAUs	IBUs	TIME

FERMENTATION

DATE	STEP (Primary, Secondary)	START TEMP	END TEMP	# OF DAYS

DATE	FERMENTATION ADDITION (Dry Hop/Fruit/Etc.)	AMOUNT	# OF DAYS

BREWING NOTES

RECIPE NAME

BREW DATE		BOTTLING/KEG DATE	
STYLE		RECIPE SIZE	
ORIGINAL GRAVITY		BITTERNESS (IBUs)	
FINAL GRAVITY		COLOR (SRM)	
BATCH SIZE		BATCH TYPE	
ALCOHOL (ABV)		EFFICIENCY	

INGREDIENTS

AMT	GRAIN/EXTRACT	ANT (Oz/g)	HOPS	TIME	% AA	IBU

Yeast Strain_____# of Packets_____

BOIL

WEIGHT	HOPS/BOIL INGREDIENTS	AAUs	IBUs	TIME

FERMENTATION

DATE	STEP (Primary, Secondary)	START TEMP	END TEMP	# OF DAYS

DATE	FERMENTATION ADDITION (Dry Hop/Fruit/Etc.)	AMOUNT	# OF DAYS

BREWING NOTES

RECIPE NAME

BREW DATE	BOTTLING/KEG DATE
STYLE	RECIPE SIZE
ORIGINAL GRAVITY	BITTERNESS (IBUs)
FINAL GRAVITY	COLOR (SRM)
BATCH SIZE	BATCH TYPE
ALCOHOL (ABV)	EFFICIENCY

INGREDIENTS

AMT	GRAIN/EXTRACT	ANT (Oz/g)	HOPS	TIME	% AA	IBU

Yeast Strain_____# of Packets_____

BOIL

WEIGHT	HOPS/BOIL INGREDIENTS	AAUs	IBUs	TIME

FERMENTATION

DATE	STEP (Primary, Secondary)	START TEMP	END TEMP	# OF DAYS

DATE	FERMENTATION ADDITION (Dry Hop/Fruit/Etc.)	AMOUNT	# OF DAYS

BREWING NOTES

RECIPE NAME

BREW DATE	BOTTLING/KEG DATE
STYLE	RECIPE SIZE
ORIGINAL GRAVITY	BITTERNESS (IBUs)
FINAL GRAVITY	COLOR (SRM)
BATCH SIZE	BATCH TYPE
ALCOHOL (ABV)	EFFICIENCY

INGREDIENTS

AMT	GRAIN/EXTRACT	ANT (Oz/g)	HOPS	TIME	% AA	IBU

Yeast Strain_____# of Packets_____

BOIL

WEIGHT	HOPS/BOIL INGREDIENTS	AAUs	IBUs	TIME

FERMENTATION

DATE	STEP (Primary, Secondary)	START TEMP	END TEMP	# OF DAYS

DATE	FERMENTATION ADDITION (Dry Hop/Fruit/Etc.)	AMOUNT	# OF DAYS

BREWING NOTES

RECIPE NAME

BREW DATE	BOTTLING/KEG DATE
STYLE	RECIPE SIZE
ORIGINAL GRAVITY	BITTERNESS (IBUs)
FINAL GRAVITY	COLOR (SRM)
BATCH SIZE	BATCH TYPE
ALCOHOL (ABV)	EFFICIENCY

INGREDIENTS

AMT	GRAIN/EXTRACT	ANT (Oz/g)	HOPS	TIME	% AA	IBU

Yeast Strain_____# of Packets_____

BOIL

WEIGHT	HOPS/BOIL INGREDIENTS	AAUs	IBUs	TIME

FERMENTATION

DATE	STEP (Primary, Secondary)	START TEMP	END TEMP	# OF DAYS

DATE	FERMENTATION ADDIT ON (Dry Hop/Fruit/Etc.)	AMOUNT	# OF DAYS

BREWING NOTES

RECIPE NAME

BREW DATE	BOTTLING/KEG DATE
STYLE	RECIPE SIZE
ORIGINAL GRAVITY	BITTERNESS (IBUs)
FINAL GRAVITY	COLOR (SRM)
BATCH SIZE	BATCH TYPE
ALCOHOL (ABV)	EFFICIENCY

INGREDIENTS

AMT	GRAIN/EXTRACT	ANT (Oz/g)	HOPS	TIME	% AA	IBU

Yeast Strain_____# of Packets_____

BOIL

WEIGHT	HOPS/BOIL INGREDIENTS	AAUs	IBUs	TIME

FERMENTATION

DATE	STEP (Primary, Secondary)	START TEMP	END TEMP	# OF DAYS

DATE	FERMENTATION ADDITION (Dry Hop/Fruit/Etc.)	AMOUNT	# OF DAYS

BREWING NOTES

RECIPE NAME

BREW DATE	BOTTLING/KEG DATE
STYLE	RECIPE SIZE
ORIGINAL GRAVITY	BITTERNESS (IBUs)
FINAL GRAVITY	COLOR (SRM)
BATCH SIZE	BATCH TYPE
ALCOHOL (ABV)	EFFICIENCY

INGREDIENTS

AMT	GRAIN/EXTRACT	ANT (Oz/g)	HOPS	TIME	% AA	IBU

Yeast Strain_____# of Packets_____

BOIL

WEIGHT	HOPS/BOIL INGREDIENTS	AAUs	IBUs	TIME

FERMENTATION

DATE	STEP (Primary, Secondary)	START TEMP	END TEMP	# OF DAYS

DATE	FERMENTATION ADDITION (Dry Hop/Fruit/Etc.)	AMOUNT	# OF DAYS

BREWING NOTES

RECIPE NAME

BREW DATE	BOTTLING/KEG DATE
STYLE	RECIPE SIZE
ORIGINAL GRAVITY	BITTERNESS (IBUs)
FINAL GRAVITY	COLOR (SRM)
BATCH SIZE	BATCH TYPE
ALCOHOL (ABV)	EFFICIENCY

INGREDIENTS

AMT	GRAIN/EXTRACT	AMT (Oz/g)	HOPS	TIME	% AA	IBU

Yeast Strain_____# of Packets_____

BOIL

WEIGHT	HOPS/BOIL INGREDIENTS	AAUs	IBUs	TIME

FERMENTATION

DATE	STEP (Primary, Secondary)	START TEMP	END TEMP	# OF DAYS

DATE	FERMENTATION ADDITION (Dry Hop/Fruit/Etc.)	AMOUNT	# OF DAYS

BREWING NOTES

RECIPE NAME

BREW DATE	BOTTLING/KEG DATE
STYLE	RECIPE SIZE
ORIGINAL GRAVITY	BITTERNESS (IBUs)
FINAL GRAVITY	COLOR (SRM)
BATCH SIZE	BATCH TYPE
ALCOHOL (ABV)	EFFICIENCY

INGREDIENTS

AMT	GRAIN/EXTRACT	ANT (Oz/g)	HOPS	TIME	% AA	IBU

Yeast Strain_____# of Packets_____

BOIL

WEIGHT	HOPS/BOIL INGREDIENTS	AAUs	IBUs	TIME

FERMENTATION

DATE	STEP (Primary, Secondary)	START TEMP	END TEMP	# OF DAYS

DATE	FERMENTATION ADDITION (Dry Hop/Fruit/Etc.)	AMOUNT	# OF DAYS

BREWING NOTES

RECIPE NAME

BREW DATE	BOTTLING/KEG DATE
STYLE	RECIPE SIZE
ORIGINAL GRAVITY	BITTERNESS (IBUs)
FINAL GRAVITY	COLOR (SRM)
BATCH SIZE	BATCH TYPE
ALCOHOL (ABV)	EFFICIENCY

INGREDIENTS

AMT	GRAIN/EXTRACT	ANT (Oz/g)	HOPS	TIME	% AA	IBU

Yeast Strain_____# of Packets_____

BOIL

WEIGHT	HOPS/BOIL INGREDIENTS	AAUs	IBUs	TIME

FERMENTATION

DATE	STEP (Primary, Secondary)	START TEMP	END TEMP	# OF DAYS

DATE	FERMENTATION ADDITION (Dry Hop/Fruit/Etc.)	AMOUNT	# OF DAYS

BREWING NOTES

RECIPE NAME

BREW DATE	BOTTLING/KEG DATE
STYLE	RECIPE SIZE
ORIGINAL GRAVITY	BITTERNESS (IBUs)
FINAL GRAVITY	COLOR (SRM)
BATCH SIZE	BATCH TYPE
ALCOHOL (ABV)	EFFICIENCY

INGREDIENTS

AMT	GRAIN/EXTRACT	ANT (Oz/g)	HOPS	TIME	% AA	IBU

Yeast Strain_____# of Packets_____

BOIL

WEIGHT	HOPS/BOIL INGREDIENTS	AAUs	IBUs	TIME

FERMENTATION

DATE	STEP (Primary, Secondary)	START TEMP	END TEMP	# OF DAYS

DATE	FERMENTATION ADDITION (Dry Hop/Fruit/Etc.)	AMOUNT	# OF DAYS

BREWING NOTES

RECIPE NAME

BREW DATE	BOTTLING/KEG DATE
STYLE	RECIPE SIZE
ORIGINAL GRAVITY	BITTERNESS (IBUs)
FINAL GRAVITY	COLOR (SRM)
BATCH SIZE	BATCH TYPE
ALCOHOL (ABV)	EFFICIENCY

INGREDIENTS

AMT	GRAIN/EXTRACT	ANT (Oz/g)	HOPS	TIME	% AA	IBU

Yeast Strain_____# of Packets_____

BOIL

WEIGHT	HOPS/BOIL INGREDIENTS	AAUs	IBUs	TIME

FERMENTATION

DATE	STEP (Primary, Secondary)	START TEMP	END TEMP	# OF DAYS

DATE	FERMENTATION ADDITION (Dry Hop/Fruit/Etc.)	AMOUNT	# OF DAYS

BREWING NOTES

RECIPE NAME

BREW DATE	BOTTLING/KEG DATE
STYLE	RECIPE SIZE
ORIGINAL GRAVITY	BITTERNESS (IBUs)
FINAL GRAVITY	COLOR (SRM)
BATCH SIZE	BATCH TYPE
ALCOHOL (ABV)	EFFICIENCY

INGREDIENTS

AMT	GRAIN/EXTRACT	ANT (Oz/g)	HOPS	TIME	% AA	IBU

Yeast Strain_____# of Packets_____

BOIL

WEIGHT	HOPS/BOIL INGREDIENTS	AAUs	IBUs	TIME

FERMENTATION

DATE	STEP (Primary, Secondary)	START TEMP	END TEMP	# OF DAYS

DATE	FERMENTATION ADDITION (Dry Hop/Fruit/Etc.)	AMOUNT	# OF DAYS

BREWING NOTES

RECIPE NAME

BREW DATE	BOTTLING/KEG DATE
STYLE	RECIPE SIZE
ORIGINAL GRAVITY	BITTERNESS (IBUs)
FINAL GRAVITY	COLOR (SRM)
BATCH SIZE	BATCH TYPE
ALCOHOL (ABV)	EFFICIENCY

INGREDIENTS

AMT	GRAIN/EXTRACT	ANT (Oz/g)	HOPS	TIME	% AA	IBU

Yeast Strain_____# of Packets_____

BOIL

WEIGHT	HOPS/BOIL INGREDIENTS	AAUs	IBUs	TIME

FERMENTATION

DATE	STEP (Primary, Secondary)	START TEMP	END TEMP	# OF DAYS

DATE	FERMENTATION ADDITION (Dry Hop/Fruit/Etc.)	AMOUNT	# OF DAYS

BREWING NOTES

RECIPE NAME

BREW DATE	BOTTLING/KEG DATE
STYLE	RECIPE SIZE
ORIGINAL GRAVITY	BITTERNESS (IBUs)
FINAL GRAVITY	COLOR (SRM)
BATCH SIZE	BATCH TYPE
ALCOHOL (ABV)	EFFICIENCY

INGREDIENTS

AMT	GRAIN/EXTRACT	ANT (Oz/g)	HOPS	TIME	% AA	IBU

Yeast Strain_____# of Packets_____

BOIL

WEIGHT	HOPS/BOIL INGREDIENTS	AAUs	IBUs	TIME

FERMENTATION

DATE	STEP (Primary, Secondary)	START TEMP	END TEMP	# OF DAYS

DATE	FERMENTATION ADDITION (Dry Hop/Fruit/Etc.)	AMOUNT	# OF DAYS

BREWING NOTES

www.ingramcontent.com/pod-product-compliance
Lightning Source LLC
LaVergne TN
LVHW020429080526
838202LV00055B/5098